EMMANUEL JOSEPH

Wear the Change, A Journey Through
Ethical Fashion and Ecological Innovation

Copyright © 2025 by Emmanuel Joseph

All rights reserved. No part of this publication may be reproduced, stored or transmitted in any form or by any means, electronic, mechanical, photocopying, recording, scanning, or otherwise without written permission from the publisher. It is illegal to copy this book, post it to a website, or distribute it by any other means without permission.

First edition

This book was professionally typeset on Reedsy.
Find out more at reedsy.com

Contents

1	Chapter 1: The Awakening of Consciousness	1
2	Chapter 2: The True Cost of Fast Fashion	3
3	Chapter 3: Sustainable Fabrics and Materials	5
4	Chapter 4: Ethical Manufacturing Practices	7
5	Chapter 5: The Role of Technology in Fashion Innovation	9
6	Chapter 6: Circular Fashion and the Future of Consumption	11
7	Chapter 7: The Power of Consumer Choices	13
8	Chapter 8: The Intersection of Fashion and Culture	15
9	Chapter 9: The Business of Ethical Fashion	17
10	Chapter 10: Fashion and Social Justice	19
11	Chapter 11: The Role of Education in Ethical Fashion	21
12	Chapter 12: The Impact of Legislation and Policy	23
13	Chapter 13: Innovations in Textile Recycling and Waste...	25
14	Chapter 14: The Future of Ethical Fashion	27
15	Chapter 15: Case Studies of Ethical Fashion Brands	29
16	Chapter 16: The Role of Media and Influencers	31
17	Chapter 17: A Call to Action	33

1

Chapter 1: The Awakening of Consciousness

In the early days of fashion, the allure of vibrant fabrics and cutting-edge designs often overshadowed the environmental and ethical implications of the industry. Our journey begins with a collective awakening—when consumers and creators alike started questioning the true cost of their garments. The realization that fashion's glamour came with a hefty price tag for both the planet and marginalized communities sparked a movement toward conscious consumption. The global conversation shifted towards sustainability, driving people to seek alternatives that aligned with their values.

Ethical fashion emerged as a beacon of hope, promising a new way to indulge in style without compromising principles. Brands began to pivot, focusing on transparency, fair wages, and environmentally-friendly materials. It wasn't an overnight revolution, but rather a gradual shift fueled by passionate advocates who believed in the power of informed choices. As this chapter unfolds, we'll explore the pivotal moments that catalyzed this change, setting the stage for a deeper understanding of ethical fashion.

Parallel to the fashion industry's awakening was a broader societal shift towards ecological awareness. The 21st century witnessed unprecedented environmental challenges—climate change, deforestation, and pollution—

prompting a reevaluation of our lifestyles. The fashion industry, as one of the largest polluters, couldn't remain indifferent. This convergence of ethical and ecological consciousness laid the groundwork for innovative solutions that would redefine the fashion landscape.

In this chapter, we'll delve into the stories of early trailblazers who dared to challenge the status quo. From grassroots movements to high-profile campaigns, their efforts ignited a fire that would transform the fashion industry. The stage is set for a transformative journey—a quest to align fashion with the values of justice, sustainability, and innovation.

2

Chapter 2: The True Cost of Fast Fashion

Fast fashion's rapid rise was fueled by a relentless pursuit of trends and low-cost production. However, beneath the surface of affordable prices and quick turnover lay a complex web of exploitation and environmental degradation. This chapter exposes the hidden costs of fast fashion, shedding light on the dark realities often overlooked by mainstream consumers. The exploitation of labor in developing countries, coupled with the vast environmental footprint of textile production, paints a grim picture of the industry's impact.

As we navigate through the murky waters of fast fashion, we'll uncover the stories of garment workers toiling in hazardous conditions for meager wages. Their plight serves as a stark reminder of the human cost embedded in our clothing. The chapter also examines the environmental toll of fast fashion, from excessive water usage and pollution to the massive amounts of waste generated by discarded garments. These revelations challenge readers to reconsider their consumption habits and the true value of their clothing.

The ethical dilemmas posed by fast fashion extend beyond labor and environmental issues. The chapter explores the psychological impact of a culture obsessed with constant novelty and disposable fashion. The pressure to keep up with ever-changing trends fosters a sense of disconnection from the craftsmanship and artistry behind each piece of clothing. By understanding the multifaceted consequences of fast fashion, readers are empowered to make more conscious and meaningful choices in their wardrobes.

Ultimately, this chapter serves as a wake-up call—a call to action for consumers, brands, and policymakers to address the systemic issues within the fashion industry. By unmasking the true cost of fast fashion, we pave the way for a more sustainable and equitable future. The journey towards ethical fashion begins with awareness and a commitment to change.

3

Chapter 3: Sustainable Fabrics and Materials

The quest for sustainability in fashion hinges on the materials we choose to create our garments. This chapter delves into the world of sustainable fabrics and materials, exploring innovative alternatives to conventional textiles. From organic cotton and hemp to recycled polyester and biodegradable fibers, the options are as diverse as they are promising. These materials not only reduce the environmental impact of fashion but also offer unique qualities that enhance the overall wearability and longevity of clothing.

Organic cotton, for instance, is grown without the use of harmful pesticides and synthetic fertilizers, resulting in a lower environmental footprint. Hemp, with its fast growth rate and minimal water requirements, is another eco-friendly alternative gaining popularity. Recycled polyester, made from post-consumer plastic waste, provides a second life for discarded materials while reducing the demand for virgin resources. The chapter also explores emerging innovations such as lab-grown fabrics and mycelium leather, which push the boundaries of sustainable fashion.

Beyond the environmental benefits, sustainable materials often come with a story—a narrative of conscious choices and ethical practices. The chapter highlights brands and designers who prioritize transparency and traceability in their supply chains, ensuring that their materials are sourced responsibly. By showcasing the journey from raw material to finished product, we gain a deeper appreciation for the efforts involved in creating truly sustainable fashion.

The adoption of sustainable materials is not without its challenges. The chapter addresses issues such as cost, scalability, and consumer perception, which can hinder widespread adoption. However, by fostering collaboration between industry stakeholders, researchers, and consumers, we can overcome these barriers and accelerate the transition to a more sustainable fashion ecosystem. The journey through sustainable fabrics and materials is a testament to the power of innovation and collective action.

4

Chapter 4: Ethical Manufacturing Practices

Ethical fashion extends beyond the choice of materials to encompass the entire manufacturing process. This chapter explores the principles of ethical manufacturing, from fair labor practices and safe working conditions to the reduction of waste and resource efficiency. By examining case studies of brands that prioritize ethical production, we gain insights into the positive impact that conscientious manufacturing can have on both people and the planet.

Fair labor practices are at the heart of ethical manufacturing. The chapter delves into the importance of providing fair wages, reasonable working hours, and safe environments for garment workers. Brands that commit to these principles contribute to the empowerment and well-being of their employees, fostering a sense of dignity and respect. The chapter also discusses the role of certifications and standards, such as Fair Trade and SA8000, in ensuring accountability and transparency in the supply chain.

Reducing waste and minimizing the environmental footprint of manufacturing is another key aspect of ethical fashion. The chapter explores innovative approaches to resource efficiency, such as zero-waste design, upcycling, and closed-loop systems. By maximizing the use of materials and reducing waste, brands can significantly lower their environmental impact.

The chapter also highlights the importance of sustainable practices in dyeing, printing, and finishing processes, which often involve harmful chemicals and excessive water usage.

Ethical manufacturing is a collaborative effort that requires the commitment of brands, suppliers, and consumers. The chapter emphasizes the role of consumers in driving demand for ethically produced garments and supporting brands that prioritize ethical practices. By choosing to support ethical fashion, consumers can contribute to a positive ripple effect throughout the industry, encouraging more brands to adopt responsible manufacturing practices. The journey through ethical manufacturing is a testament to the power of collective action and the potential for positive change.

5

Chapter 5: The Role of Technology in Fashion Innovation

Technology has always been a driving force in the fashion industry, and its role in promoting sustainability and ethics is no exception. This chapter explores the ways in which technological advancements are revolutionizing the fashion landscape, from 3D printing and digital design to blockchain and artificial intelligence. These innovations not only enhance the creative process but also offer solutions to some of the industry's most pressing challenges.

3D printing, for example, allows designers to create intricate and customizable garments with minimal waste. By producing only what is needed, 3D printing reduces the excess inventory and overproduction that plagues traditional manufacturing. Digital design tools enable designers to experiment with virtual prototypes, reducing the need for physical samples and saving valuable resources. These technologies also open up new possibilities for creativity and customization, allowing consumers to have a more personalized and sustainable fashion experience.

Blockchain technology offers transparency and traceability in the supply chain, addressing the issue of opaque and unethical practices. By providing a secure and immutable record of transactions, blockchain ensures that every step of the production process is documented and verifiable. This level of transparency empowers consumers to make informed choices and hold brands accountable for their practices. The chapter also explores the potential of artificial intelligence in optimizing supply chains, predicting trends, and reducing waste.

The integration of technology into the fashion industry is not without its challenges. The chapter addresses concerns such as data privacy, the digital divide, and the environmental impact of electronic waste. However, by embracing responsible and ethical technological practices, the fashion industry can harness the power of innovation to drive positive change. The journey through technology and fashion innovation is a testament to the transformative potential of human ingenuity and collaboration.

6

Chapter 6: Circular Fashion and the Future of Consumption

The concept of circular fashion offers a radical departure from the traditional linear model of production and consumption. This chapter explores the principles of circularity, which prioritize resource efficiency, waste reduction, and the continuous use of materials. By designing garments for longevity, repairability, and recyclability, circular fashion aims to create a closed-loop system that minimizes environmental impact and extends the life cycle of products.

At the heart of circular fashion is the idea of designing for longevity. The chapter discusses the importance of creating high-quality, durable garments that withstand the test of time. By prioritizing craftsmanship and timeless design, brands can encourage consumers to invest in pieces that they will cherish for years to come. The chapter also explores the role of repair and maintenance, highlighting the resurgence of skills such as mending, tailoring, and upcycling as essential components of a circular fashion system.

Recycling and upcycling are key strategies in the circular fashion model. The chapter examines innovative approaches to textile recycling, from mechanical and chemical processes to creative upcycling techniques. By transforming old garments into new products, brands can reduce the demand for virgin materials and divert textiles from landfills. The chapter also explores the potential of circular business models, such as clothing rental, resale, and take-back programs, which offer consumers alternatives to traditional ownership.

The transition to circular fashion requires a fundamental shift in consumer behavior and industry practices. The chapter emphasizes the importance of collaboration between designers, brands, policymakers, and consumers in creating a circular economy. By embracing circular principles, a paradigm shift in attitudes and practices is essential. By fostering a culture of responsibility and innovation, we can create a fashion industry that is not only sustainable but also regenerative.

7

Chapter 7: The Power of Consumer Choices

Consumer choices wield immense power in shaping the fashion industry. This chapter delves into the role of consumers as agents of change, exploring how individual actions and collective movements can drive the shift toward ethical and sustainable fashion. From supporting ethical brands to adopting mindful consumption practices, the chapter highlights the various ways in which consumers can make a positive impact.

The rise of conscious consumerism is fueled by a growing awareness of the ethical and environmental implications of fashion. The chapter examines the influence of social media, documentaries, and advocacy campaigns in raising awareness and mobilizing consumers. By sharing stories of consumers who have embraced sustainable fashion, we illustrate the ripple effect of individual choices and the potential for widespread change.

Mindful consumption practices are at the heart of ethical fashion. The chapter provides practical tips and strategies for building a sustainable wardrobe, such as choosing quality over quantity, investing in timeless pieces, and prioritizing second-hand and vintage clothing. By shifting the focus from fast fashion to thoughtful curation, consumers can create wardrobes that reflect their values and stand the test of time.

The chapter also explores the role of community and collaboration in driving change. From clothing swaps and repair workshops to online platforms and social movements, consumers are finding innovative ways to support each other and amplify their impact. By fostering a sense of community and shared purpose, we can create a fashion ecosystem that is inclusive, resilient, and sustainable.

8

Chapter 8: The Intersection of Fashion and Culture

Fashion is a powerful cultural force that reflects and shapes societal values. This chapter explores the intersection of fashion and culture, examining how clothing serves as a medium of expression, identity, and social change. From traditional textiles and indigenous practices to contemporary movements and subcultures, we uncover the rich tapestry of cultural influences that define ethical fashion.

The chapter delves into the significance of traditional textiles and craftsmanship, highlighting the importance of preserving cultural heritage and supporting indigenous artisans. By celebrating the artistry and wisdom embedded in traditional practices, we can foster a deeper appreciation for the cultural dimensions of fashion. The chapter also discusses the role of cultural appropriation and the need for respect and collaboration in the fashion industry.

Contemporary fashion movements and subcultures play a crucial role in challenging norms and driving social change. The chapter explores the influence of movements such as punk, hip-hop, and streetwear in pushing the boundaries of fashion and advocating for inclusivity and diversity. By amplifying the voices of marginalized communities and promoting representation, these movements contribute to a more equitable and vibrant fashion landscape.

The chapter also examines the role of fashion in activism and advocacy. From slogan tees and protest fashion to eco-conscious collections and ethical collaborations, fashion has become a powerful tool for raising awareness and driving change. By harnessing the power of fashion as a cultural and social force, we can inspire collective action and create a more just and sustainable world.

9

Chapter 9: The Business of Ethical Fashion

Ethical fashion is not only a moral imperative but also a viable business model. This chapter explores the economic dimensions of ethical fashion, from sustainable entrepreneurship and ethical supply chains to innovative business models and market trends. By examining case studies of successful ethical brands, we gain insights into the strategies and principles that drive sustainable business practices.

Sustainable entrepreneurship is at the forefront of the ethical fashion movement. The chapter highlights the stories of visionary entrepreneurs who have built businesses that prioritize people, planet, and profit. From ethical sourcing and transparent supply chains to circular design and zero-waste production, these entrepreneurs are redefining the fashion industry and setting new standards for sustainability.

Ethical supply chains are a cornerstone of sustainable business practices. The chapter explores the importance of building relationships with suppliers, ensuring fair wages and safe working conditions, and minimizing environmental impact. By adopting a holistic approach to supply chain management, brands can create a positive impact throughout the entire production process.

Innovative business models are driving the growth of ethical fashion. The chapter examines the rise of direct-to-consumer brands, subscription services, and digital platforms that prioritize sustainability and transparency. By leveraging technology and embracing new business models, ethical fashion brands can reach a wider audience and drive systemic change in the industry.

The chapter also discusses the role of consumers in supporting ethical businesses. By choosing to invest in brands that align with their values, consumers can drive demand for sustainable products and create a positive feedback loop. The journey through the business of ethical fashion is a testament to the potential for innovation, collaboration, and sustainable growth.

10

Chapter 10: Fashion and Social Justice

The fashion industry has a significant impact on social justice, from labor rights and gender equality to representation and inclusivity. This chapter explores the intersection of fashion and social justice, highlighting the importance of creating an industry that is fair, equitable, and inclusive. By examining the challenges and opportunities for social change, we gain insights into the role of fashion in promoting justice and equality.

Labor rights are a critical issue in the fashion industry. The chapter delves into the importance of fair wages, safe working conditions, and the right to collective bargaining for garment workers. By supporting ethical labor practices and advocating for workers' rights, we can create a fashion industry that respects and empowers its workforce.

Gender equality is another key aspect of social justice in fashion. The chapter explores the role of fashion in challenging gender norms and promoting inclusivity. From gender-neutral collections and diverse representation to women-led businesses and feminist movements, fashion has the power to drive gender equality and amplify marginalized voices.

Representation and inclusivity are essential for a just and equitable fashion industry. The chapter discusses the importance of diverse representation in fashion campaigns, runways, and leadership positions. By promoting inclusivity and celebrating diversity, we can create a fashion industry that reflects and respects the rich tapestry of human experiences.

The chapter also examines the role of fashion in activism and advocacy. From ethical collaborations and cause-driven collections to awareness campaigns and grassroots movements, fashion has become a powerful tool for social change. By harnessing the power of fashion to promote justice and equality, we can create a more inclusive and equitable world.

11

Chapter 11: The Role of Education in Ethical Fashion

Education plays a vital role in driving the ethical fashion movement. This chapter explores the importance of education in raising awareness, fostering innovation, and building a more sustainable and equitable fashion industry. By examining the role of schools, universities, and professional organizations, we gain insights into the ways in which education can empower the next generation of fashion leaders.

The chapter highlights the role of fashion schools and universities in shaping the future of the industry. By incorporating sustainability and ethics into their curricula, these institutions are equipping students with the knowledge and skills needed to drive positive change. The chapter also discusses the importance of interdisciplinary approaches, which integrate fashion with fields such as environmental science, social justice, and business.

Professional organizations and industry initiatives play a crucial role in promoting ethical fashion education. The chapter explores the efforts of organizations such as the Sustainable Apparel Coalition, the Ethical Fashion Forum, and Fashion Revolution in providing resources, training, and advocacy for ethical fashion. By fostering a culture of continuous learning and collaboration, these organizations are driving systemic change in the industry.

The chapter also examines the role of consumer education in promoting ethical fashion. From awareness campaigns and educational resources to workshops and community events, consumers are being empowered to make informed choices and support ethical brands. By raising awareness and providing practical tools, education can inspire collective action and create a more sustainable fashion ecosystem.

12

Chapter 12: The Impact of Legislation and Policy

Legislation and policy play a critical role in shaping the fashion industry and promoting ethical practices. This chapter explores the impact of government regulations, international agreements, and industry standards in driving sustainability and social justice. By examining case studies of successful policy interventions, we gain insights into the ways in which legislation can create a more accountable and transparent fashion industry.

The chapter discusses the role of government regulations in addressing environmental and social issues in the fashion industry. From labor laws and environmental standards to waste management and circular economy policies, governments have the power to set the rules and create incentives for ethical practices. The chapter also highlights the importance of enforcement and accountability in ensuring that regulations are effective.

International agreements and initiatives play a crucial role in promoting ethical fashion. The chapter explores the impact of agreements such as the Paris Agreement, the United Nations Sustainable Development Goals, and the Bangladesh Accord on Fire and Building Safety. By fostering global collaboration and setting common standards, these initiatives can drive systemic change and create a more sustainable fashion industry.

Industry standards and certifications are essential for promoting ethical practices and ensuring transparency. The chapter examines the role of standards such as Fair Trade, GOTS (Global Organic Textile Standard), and the Higg Index in providing benchmarks for sustainability and social responsibility. By adopting and promoting these standards, brands can build trust with consumers and demonstrate their commitment to ethical practices.

The chapter also discusses the role of advocacy and activism in shaping policy and legislation. From grassroots movements and consumer campaigns to industry coalitions and lobbying efforts, advocates play a crucial role in driving policy change and holding brands accountable. By harnessing the power of collective action, we can create a fashion industry that is fair, transparent, and sustainable.

13

Chapter 13: Innovations in Textile Recycling and Waste Reduction

The fashion industry is one of the largest contributors to waste, but innovative solutions are emerging to address this challenge. This chapter explores the advancements in textile recycling and waste reduction, highlighting the potential for a more circular and sustainable fashion industry. From mechanical and chemical recycling to upcycling and zero-waste design, we uncover the cutting-edge technologies and practices that are transforming waste into valuable resources.

Mechanical recycling involves the physical processing of textiles to create new fibers or materials. The chapter delves into the techniques and technologies used in mechanical recycling, such as shredding, carding, and spinning. By converting old garments into new fibers, mechanical recycling reduces the demand for virgin materials and diverts textiles from landfills. The chapter also discusses the challenges and limitations of mechanical recycling, such as fiber quality degradation and contamination. Despite these challenges, mechanical recycling remains a promising solution for transforming textile waste into valuable resources.

Chemical recycling, on the other hand, involves breaking down textiles into their molecular components to create new fibers or materials. This chapter explores the various chemical recycling processes, such as depolymerization and solvolysis, which can convert synthetic fibers like polyester back into their original monomers. Chemical recycling offers the potential for higher-quality recycled fibers and the ability to process mixed-fiber textiles. However, it also presents challenges related to energy consumption, chemical usage, and scalability.

Upcycling is another innovative approach to waste reduction, transforming discarded garments and textiles into new and unique products. The chapter highlights the creativity and resourcefulness of designers who embrace upcycling, turning waste into fashion statements. By reimagining and repurposing existing materials, upcycling reduces the demand for virgin resources and extends the life cycle of textiles.

Zero-waste design is a holistic approach to fashion that aims to eliminate waste at every stage of the production process. The chapter examines the principles of zero-waste design, such as pattern-making techniques that maximize fabric utilization and design strategies that minimize offcuts. By prioritizing resource efficiency and waste reduction, zero-waste design offers a sustainable alternative to traditional fashion practices.

14

Chapter 14: The Future of Ethical Fashion

The journey through ethical fashion and ecological innovation culminates in this chapter, which envisions the future of the fashion industry. By examining emerging trends, technologies, and consumer behaviors, we gain insights into the potential for a more sustainable, ethical, and inclusive fashion landscape. This chapter serves as a call to action, inspiring readers to become active participants in shaping the future of fashion.

The chapter explores the rise of slow fashion, a movement that prioritizes quality, craftsmanship, and sustainability over speed and volume. Slow fashion encourages consumers to invest in timeless pieces that are made to last, fostering a deeper connection to their clothing and the people who make it. By embracing slow fashion principles, we can create a more mindful and responsible fashion culture.

Technological advancements will continue to play a crucial role in driving ethical fashion. The chapter delves into the potential of innovations such as biofabrication, smart textiles, and digital fashion. These technologies offer exciting possibilities for creating sustainable and customizable garments that align with the values of the modern consumer.

Consumer behavior will also shape the future of ethical fashion. The chapter examines the growing demand for transparency, accountability, and sustainability in the fashion industry. By supporting ethical brands and adopting mindful consumption practices, consumers can drive positive change and create a more equitable and sustainable fashion ecosystem.

The chapter concludes with a vision for the future of ethical fashion—one that is inclusive, resilient, and regenerative. By fostering a culture of innovation, collaboration, and responsibility, we can create a fashion industry that not only meets the needs of today but also ensures a thriving planet for future generations.

15

Chapter 15: Case Studies of Ethical Fashion Brands

To bring the concepts of ethical fashion to life, this chapter presents case studies of pioneering brands that have successfully integrated sustainability and ethics into their business models. These stories of innovation and resilience offer valuable insights and inspiration for aspiring entrepreneurs, designers, and consumers alike.

The chapter highlights the journey of brands such as Patagonia, known for its commitment to environmental activism and transparent supply chains. By prioritizing sustainability and advocating for systemic change, Patagonia has set a high standard for ethical business practices. The chapter also explores the story of Stella McCartney, a luxury brand that has embraced sustainable materials and cruelty-free practices while maintaining a strong design ethos.

Other case studies include brands like Everlane, which focuses on radical transparency and ethical production, and Eileen Fisher, known for its circular design initiatives and commitment to social justice. These brands demonstrate that it is possible to build successful and profitable businesses while prioritizing sustainability, ethics, and social impact.

The chapter also features emerging brands that are pushing the boundaries of innovation and creativity. From startups developing lab-grown leather to designers creating garments from recycled ocean plastics, these brands represent the future of ethical fashion. By showcasing their achievements and challenges, we gain a deeper understanding of the potential and possibilities within the ethical fashion movement.

16

Chapter 16: The Role of Media and Influencers

Media and influencers play a significant role in shaping public perception and driving the ethical fashion movement. This chapter explores the impact of media coverage, social media platforms, and influencer partnerships in raising awareness and inspiring action. By examining the strategies and stories of influential figures in the ethical fashion space, we gain insights into the power of communication and advocacy.

The chapter delves into the role of documentaries, films, and investigative journalism in exposing the realities of the fashion industry and advocating for change. Films like "The True Cost" and "RiverBlue" have played a pivotal role in raising awareness about the environmental and social impacts of fashion. By shining a light on these issues, media coverage can inspire consumers to make more conscious choices and hold brands accountable.

Social media platforms have become powerful tools for advocacy and education. The chapter explores how influencers, bloggers, and activists use their platforms to promote ethical fashion, share resources, and connect with like-minded communities. By leveraging their reach and influence, these individuals can drive conversations, challenge norms, and inspire collective action.

The chapter also examines the importance of collaboration between brands and influencers. Ethical fashion brands often partner with influencers who share their values and can authentically represent their mission. These partnerships can help amplify the message of sustainability and ethics, reaching a wider audience and creating a positive impact.

Ultimately, the role of media and influencers is to inform, inspire, and mobilize. By harnessing the power of communication and storytelling, we can create a more informed and engaged consumer base that is committed to driving positive change in the fashion industry.

17

Chapter 17: A Call to Action

The final chapter of our journey through ethical fashion and ecological innovation is a call to action. By reflecting on the lessons learned and the stories shared, we are inspired to become active participants in the movement for a more sustainable and ethical fashion industry. This chapter serves as a guide for readers, offering practical steps and strategies to make a positive impact.

The chapter emphasizes the importance of individual actions in driving systemic change. From supporting ethical brands and adopting mindful consumption practices to advocating for policy change and participating in community initiatives, every action counts. By making conscious choices and using our voices, we can contribute to a more equitable and sustainable fashion ecosystem.

Collaboration and collective action are essential for creating lasting change. The chapter encourages readers to connect with like-minded individuals and organizations, participate in events and campaigns, and support initiatives that promote ethical fashion. By working together, we can amplify our impact and create a ripple effect that extends beyond our individual efforts.

Education and awareness are key components of the movement for ethical fashion. The chapter highlights the importance of staying informed, sharing knowledge, and fostering a culture of continuous learning. By educating ourselves and others, we can inspire a new generation of conscious consumers and ethical leaders.

The journey through ethical fashion and ecological innovation is ongoing, and it requires our continued commitment and passion. By embracing the principles of sustainability, ethics, and innovation, we can create a fashion industry that reflects our values and respects the planet. The future of fashion is in our hands—let's wear the change.

Wear the Change: A Journey Through Ethical Fashion and Ecological Innovation

Fashion is more than just a statement of style—it's a reflection of our values and our impact on the world. "Wear the Change: A Journey Through Ethical Fashion and Ecological Innovation" is an enlightening exploration into the world of sustainable fashion. This book delves into the transformation of the fashion industry, from the exploitation and environmental degradation of fast fashion to the rise of conscious consumption and innovative solutions.

Across 17 captivating chapters, you'll uncover the true cost of fast fashion, discover sustainable materials, and explore ethical manufacturing practices. You'll learn about the pivotal role of technology in fashion innovation and the principles of circular fashion that aim to create a closed-loop system. The power of consumer choices and the influence of cultural and social justice movements are thoroughly examined, providing insights into how individuals and communities can drive positive change.

The book also highlights the journeys of trailblazing ethical fashion brands and the importance of media and influencers in shaping public perception. With a call to action, it encourages readers to become active participants in the movement for a more sustainable and ethical fashion industry.

"Wear the Change" is not just a book—it's a manifesto for a new era of fashion where style, ethics, and sustainability coexist harmoniously. Join the journey and wear the change you wish to see in the world.

www.ingramcontent.com/pod-product-compliance
Lightning Source LLC
LaVergne TN
LVHW020500080526
838202LV00057B/6063